POLAR BABIES

POLAR BEAR CUBS

by Genevieve Nilsen

TABLE OF CONTENTS

I0807994

tadpole books

WORDS TO KNOW

cubs

hunt

play

snow

swim

white

POLAR BEAR CUBS

These are polar bear cubs.

They are white.

They blend in with snow.

They are small.

mom
Mom is big.

Mom teaches them to swim.

She teaches them to hunt.

They play!

Fun!

They grow up.

They are big.

LET'S REVIEW!

Polar bears are white. They blend in with snow. Do you think it is warm or cold where they live?

INDEX